HEAL OWN MIND

DEEPAK SHUKLA

XpressPublishing
An imprint of Notion Press

XpressPublishing
An Imprint of Notion Press

No.8, 3rd Cross Street,CIT Colony,
Mylapore, Chennai, Tamil Nadu-600004

ISBN 978-1-64951-241-3

Dedicated to everyone who wonders if i am writing
about them. I am

Contents

Foreword

In three words i can sum up everything ,
i have learned about life ,it goes on.
- ROBERT FROST

Preface

Acknowledgements

The main things i wanted to say,and thankfully it's what most people say they get out of the book ,is simply an acknnowledgement that we do affect each other in ways we can't predict.

Prologue

A SMALL THEORY

People observe the colours of the day only at its beginnings and ends,but to me it's quite clear that a day mergs through a multitude of shades and intonations,with each passing moment.A single hour can consist of thousand of different colours.waxy yellows,cloud-spat blues.murky darkness. IN my life of work , i make it a point to notice them.

Introduction

I am so tired of all the negativity around me! Are you? This world is toxic and it is sick. I hate watching the news, reading the newspaper or even interacting with my neighbors. I don't want to appear antisocial. I genuinely love people. But this world has made us cold and cruel.

The result is a society of unhappy people. Well over 50% of all marriages end in divorce. Well over 50% of all young adults do not even believe in marriage. We need to get back to the days where it was easy to talk to strangers and it was unnatural not to be polite.

Back to the days where people actually believed in love and looked out for their neighbors. We need to start loving ourselves again. We each need to be the change we wish to see in the world. We need to heal ourselves and start loving ourselves again.

Happy people are successful people. This is simply because being happy makes it easy to stay motivated to reaching your goals. Your thoughts have a very significant impact on the life you lead and the quality of the relationships you will have with family members, friends, and significant others. Some even reason that
our thoughts and beliefs can have an even stronger effect on our health than modern medicine. Consider these

examples:

• A middle-aged man dies a day after his Doctor diagnosed him with Cancer, even though his autopsy revealed he was misdiagnosed.

• Many women who are desperate to have a child will begin to have real symptoms of a pregnancy such as cravings and an increase in the size of their breasts, despite the fact that they are not actually pregnant.

• People who suffer from Depression who participate in clinical trials for new antidepressants start experiencing an improvement in their moods although they were given the placebo and not the actual drug.

That being said, it has been scientifically proven that you can improve your health, career and relationships simply by improving the way you think about yourself and the world around you. This is a lot cheaper than paying for sessions with a therapist or paying a Divorce Lawyer.

This book is intended to help you heal yourself of all the scars and the influence of all the negativity around. I guarantee that learning to rid yourself of the pain of this world will drastically improve the quality of your life from this point forward.

ONE
KNOW YOUR SELF

"The more you know yourself, the more patience you have for what you see in others." - Erik Erikson

Knowing who you are is a very crucial aspect of healing yourself. How can you avoid a disaster if you are simply floating through life with no clear sense of what you stand for, and what you refuse to tolerate?
There is a reason why the small town girl with big dreams, who gets to the big city, often ends up in some miserable and dare I say, compromising, situation.
Think too of the unhappy Doctor who is only a Doctor because his parents decided that he needed to become the first Doctor in their family. What about the hen picked mama's boy who dates a girl he cannot stand because it makes his mother happy? These three have a lot in common.

Their problem can be explained in the old saying that points out that if we do not know where we are going, any road will be the right one. And better yet, 'if we do not stand for something, we will fall for anything.' In other words, if we do not understand ourselves, this includes our hopes, dreams, and aspirations, it will be easy for just about anyone to push us into a decision we will

regret for the rest of our lives. Living down a choice you regret, especially if you have to face its consequences on a daily basis, is going to be one of the hardest things you have ever had to do. Living with the burden of these choices is part of the reason many people are so bitter and unkind. This is not the way I want you to navigate through your life.

 When we take the time to understand who we truly are, the intricacies of our own personalities, we will have the keys to unlock our true potential. You cannot become your best self if you do not know what that entails. When you understand yourself, you are more likely to end up choosing a career that you love. And it is quite easy to be passionately driven to achieve great things when you are pursuing a career that you love.

 Additionally, when you are at the top of your game, you will seek out the kind of partners and friends that will make you happy and thus bring out the best in you. They will understand the way you think and may very well think the same way you do too. These are the kind of people who will not laugh at your dreams or be jealous of your success. Being surrounded by loving, supportive people, will make you a kinder, happier and dare I say, more successful person.

Individuals who have a deep understanding of themselves, are often more decisive and optimistic. That is because these individuals are in full control of their life choices and they chose well. They are more likely to see opportunities where others see setbacks. It also takes far less effort to be productive when you enjoy what you do. Additionally, the fact that you enjoy your career will give you a competitive edge and you will not depend on the praise of others for motivation. The satisfaction of a job well done will keep you pushing forward.

I know that these may seem like ideal circumstances, where our choices are not dependent on the desires of our family and where we are all strong enough not to succumb to the pressure they will put on us to make a certain decision. But believe me, knowing and truly understanding yourself will open doors to opportunities you would have never seen coming otherwise. It will be easier for you to stand up to the pressures around you when you know without a doubt what the right decision for you will be. I am not encouraging you to shrug your responsibilities of providing for your family, I am encouraging you to understand who you are and be true to who you are at all times. You will be much happier as a result, and far easier to love, when you are not carrying the heavy weight of a bad decision around for the rest of your life.

How to Get to Know Yourself

This is easier said than done, but it is not impossible. You can start with some objective assessment. This does not mean simply asking the people around what they think of you. Your interactions with them, whether negative or positive, will prevent them from

being as objective as you need them to be. A better option would be making use of a reputable personality test. One of the popular options is the Myers-Briggs Personality type test. This test will determine which of the 16 personality types of this theory best describes who you are. It has gained popularity in recent times because its results can be used to determine the environment you work best in and even how you interact with the people around you. Plus whether you like the results or not they tend to be surprisingly accurate.

Career aptitude tests are another great option. These are designed to help you understand your skill set better and how you can use these skills to select the right career. It is never too late to start a career that you can love.

Once you have a carefully thought out plan that will allow you to care for your responsibilities and still venture into a field that you love, go for it. It might be a case that money is tight and you are already strapped for time and may not be able to make a move right now. But I would encourage you to continue preparing yourself. Keep learning all that you can about that career online or from the people around you. That way, if the opportunity should arise, you will be in a position to take it.

Once you have taken the time to learn about yourself, you may find some dirty laundry and hidden scars that you probably would have rather kept hidden. Unfortunately, you have been wearing
these scars every day in the way you interact with those around you. These scars could have made you too soft to express how you feel or too cold to care about the feelings of others. Now that you can see yourself clearly, become the best version of yourself. Love yourself. And above all else, be true to yourself. Knowing your limits is another important skill to master in order to navigate through this crazy world successfully. This will be discussed in the next chapter.

"If You Are Working On Something That You Really Care About, You Don't Have To Be Pushed. The Vision Pulls You." – Steve Jobs

TWO
KNOW THE LIMITS

"A great man is always willing to be little." — Ralph Waldo Emerson

A key aspect of the results of a Myers-Briggs Personality type test is the section which outlines your strengths and weakness. A lot of the mistakes we make and problems we encounter could have been avoided altogether if we were a little more knowledgeable about our limitations. Just think about an eager weightlifter who tries to lift too much, too soon. What do you think will happen? Any rational individual will realize that the weightlifter is going to hurt themselves. Some will argue that this illustration is encouraging us to limit ourselves, and if we do, and stop pushing ourselves, we will never know our true potential.

There is no limit to what you can achieve if you set your mind to it, and sometimes you will never know how strong you are until you try. You need to, however, ensure that reason and logic prevail when reaching out to achieve your goals. If you have never lifted 100 pounds, maybe starting with 20 pounds today would be a better idea. There is nothing wrong with thinking big, but I would encourage you to start small and work your way up. In essence, I am encouraging you to be modest in your expectations. Modesty will not only help you to avoid setting unrealistic expectations, it will also help you to set realistic time frames to achieve your goals. Many people become frustrated when they reach a certain age and have not achieved a certain goal. But just consider the contrast between Mark Zuckerberg and Colonel Sanders. Mark Zuckerberg founded his Facebook empire in his early twenty's, but Colonel Sanders did not become the founder of Kentucky Fried Chicken (KFC) until he was in his eighty's. Both men are considered highly successful, but each achieved success at different times.

Maybe it's just not your time or maybe you are just not in the right industry. As highlighted in chapter 1, choosing a career in a field you love, will help you to stay motivated and become successful. This theory is demonstrated in the lives of both of these men. Their success was as a result of a passion for something they loved.

A modest approach to life will also help you to avoid comparing your achievements to those of other people. Some people hit the ball out of the park on the first try, and there are others who have to work their way up the ladder. Some will get married right out of college, others will have to wait a few years and kiss a few frogs before they find the right person. In fact, both Mark Zuckerberg and Colonel Sanders experienced many setbacks on the way to success. You will too. Do not expect that your life will be different.

No matter what you hope to achieve, you are going to have to
work harder than you have ever worked before, and you may have to wait longer than you expected too.

The beautiful quality of modesty extends far beyond becoming successful. This is a quality that will help you to stop biting off more than you can chew. You do not need to say yes to everyone. This applies both to your personal life, and at work. Don't agree to unreasonable deadlines because you want to impress your boss, unless you are 100% sure you will be able to complete the task. If you have been given an assignment, and you are unsure about how to get it done, do not be afraid to ask for help. If you work a full-time job and have a family to take care of, don't commit to too much at your child's school. Know thy limits! This applies to your time, energy, emotions, and skills. Modesty works hand in hand with honesty, the next chapter will explain you can heal yourself and improve your life by means of this quality as well.

THREE
BE HONEST

"Honesty is the fastest way to prevent a mistake from turning into a failure." - James Altucher

The only thing worse than a liar is a thief. Liars make life difficult and often do not realize the far-reaching effects of their actions. Lying makes us unhappy people, who constantly have to be covering our tracks and watching our backs. In fact, there are few things as toxic as a liar. We should never allow the negativity in this world to force us to become dishonest people. Lying will only put you closer to the door that leads to cheating and stealing. Quit while you are ahead. Just think about the possible outcomes of a single act of dishonesty:

• Permanent damage to your reputation

• Permanent damage to your relationships
• Loss of income
• Loss of self-respect
• Permanently damaging the reputation of another individual

- Feelings of guilt
- Loss of sleep
- Loss of trust

If you research the word honesty, you find synonyms such as honor, sincerity, fairness, integrity, uprightness, virtue and truthfulness. Being honest requires more than not lying when in a difficult situation.

Being honest requires being morally upright in all things. In other words, we will try to be truthful in all things and gain the trust of those around us, by means of our actions. But honesty is a very tricky thing. It is hard to list all the areas in which we need to be honest.

A good rule of thumb if you are unsure if an act is honest or not, is whether you have to hide it or deceive someone into believing you did otherwise. If you will need to hide or cover your tracks after doing or saying something, you are probably not being honest.

The benefits of being honest far outweigh any challenges you may perceive as a result of this course. Think of the peace of mind of not having to rethink your every move or watching over your shoulder because you are constantly in fear of being found out. Imagine waking up and not being burdened by the heavy guilt
as a result of your actions. And don't be fooled into thinking that no one benefits from your honesty. It is very easy to become attracted to and to respect someone who is honest. Most employers include that quality as being of the utmost importance when seeking new recruits or considering a possible promotion of someone within their organization.

Being honest does not mean that we should volunteer all of our confidential affairs to everyone who is trying to pry into our business. Instead, we should not withhold relevant information from individuals who deserve a truthful answer.

Being honest also means avoiding the various means that will pop up to get more than we deserve or leading someone to believe something about ourselves that is not true. There are, however, times when some of us might find ourselves in very catastrophic situations because we are thought of as being too honest.

This is often the case when our words are not tempered with kindness. The next chapter will explore how that attribute can help us avoid a lot of the problems that can result from that sort of speech.

FOUR

BE KIND

"Kindness is the language which the deaf can hear and the blind can see." - Mark Twain

Being kind means being warm, considerate, gentle and friendly. To get a friend, you must be a friend. Even more cliché is the saying, 'birds of a feather, flock together.' If you want to attract happy, supportive people into your life, you need to be that kind of person. Why would anyone want to be around you otherwise?

As the wise Maya Angelou highlighted, long after the memory of the interaction has faded, people will remember how that interaction made them feel. When we are unkind, we make the lives of those around us much harder than it has to be. We make them feel unloved, underappreciated, and isolated when we are mean or unpleasant.

Would you want anyone to treat you that way? Would you enjoy such harsh treatment? Don't you think treating people that way at work, at school or in your own home, makes your life a lot harder than it has to be as well? Kindness fosters a spirit of cooperation, even among people who do not really know each other. Surrounding yourself with people who are willing to work alongside you is far easier than trying to conquer this world alone.

Being unkind envelopes a wide variety of actions. Our words are the most common form of unkindness. Being harsh, condescending or even abrupt, can be interpreted as unkind. Using your words to put others down and elevate yourself is not only unkind, it is also a very selfish act, that often causes more harm than good. A key aspect of kindness is being polite. Let us take some time to learn more about this beautiful quality.

Why Be Polite

Being polite is really not as hard as some people make it seem. While it is true that being polite is becoming increasingly difficult as a result of the negative attitudes of the people around us, it is not impossible. Being polite might inflate the ego of these individuals, but our being polite in not a reflection on them.

Our being polite reflects positively on our character, come what may. Individuals who are polite are often thought of as kind, principled, professional and pleasant. And with this very interconnected world that we live in, you just never know who you might have insulted.

Just imagine how embarrassed you will be if you show up for a job interview, only to realize that the man you just cursed in the parking lot because you think they parked in 'your' spot, is actually the interviewer. Trust me, it has happened many times before and could happen to you.

Being polite involves being respectful and considerate of the needs, feelings, time, resources, values and cultural norms, of others. Being polite and kind will make you very likable and will encourage others to reciprocate your consideration. Another benefit of being polite is that it will make it very easy for you to gain the respect of those around you.

Even if they do not instantly change their behavior, they will be forced to respect you and your standards. Eventually, they may change for the better as a result of your efforts. Wouldn't life be much easier if we all had jobs in which our employees, subordinates, and colleagues, all treated us with respect? Respect has to be earned and being polite is one of the easiest ways to earn it.

How to be Polite and Kind

1. If you have nothing kind to say, don't say it, post it on social media or even think it. Even words that are whispered to a friend have been known to turn around and bite you.

2. Don't be stingy with greetings and salutations. If you enter a room, pleasantly greet all present. When you are leavings, kindly excuse yourself. And if you are greeted, respond warmly and with a smile.

3. Do not criticize the efforts of others, especially when it is obvious that they tried very hard to accomplish a particular task. If you must offer some constructive criticism, sandwich it with some genuine commendation.

4. Be appreciative of the efforts of others. Even if what is presented is not to your liking, there is no need to make it known.

5. Try to learn a little about the cultural norms and beliefs of those around you. You do not have to share their views, you simply need to know enough not to unintentionally offend them. It is also most polite to allow them to freely express these views, without fear of being disrespected. You can always agree to disagree.

6. You do not always have to insist on things being done your way. Give someone else a chance to shine every now and then.

7. Don't monopolize conversations by speaking only about yourself and your accomplishments. Show personal interest in others by asking them about themselves and actually listening to what they have to say.

8. When someone is speaking to you, give them your full attention. Stop walking, typing or whatever else you are doing, and make eye contact. If you are busy, politely pause, evaluate how lengthy the conversations needs to be, assure them that you
value what they have to say, and then arrange a more suitable time to continue.

FIVE

BE FORGIVING

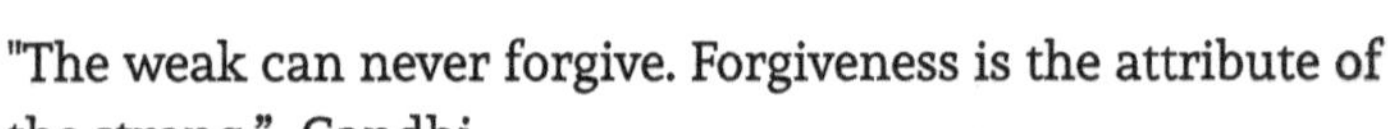

"The weak can never forgive. Forgiveness is the attribute of the strong."- Gandhi

It is not easy to forgive. The very existence of the need to use the word implies that we have been hurt in some way. Forgiving a grievance, whether real or imagined, will be one of the best gifts you can give yourself. This is so whether you believe the individual deserves such kindness or not. When we refuse to forgive, we become resentful. Holding on to resentment is like drinking poison, and expecting the individual that wronged us to suffer. It can also be compared to inflicting wounds on our own bodies, and expecting someone else to feel the pain.

This logic is not only riddled with flaws, it is also quite dangerous. Resentment can easily become hate and hatred is a very ugly thing. But why do we find it so hard to forgive? If forgiving someone who hurt us will be so beneficial, why does the very idea of letting go of the hurt make us feel so uneasy?

The real problem lies in the fact that none of us want to continue reliving the horror of whatever wrong was done to us. But as we continue to think about how badly we were hurt, we unconsciously begin to think about making the individual pay for what they did. Our flawed sense of justice often compels us to believe that if we
hold on to all the pain that was caused and refuse to let it go, we will be getting the justice we deserve.

This is especially so when the individual does not appear to be sorry for what they have done. Unfortunately, we cannot force the individual to become a better person by resentfully withholding our friendship or kindness from them. We are only hurting ourselves as we force our minds to relive the pain over and over again.

While we are angrily storming through life with the heaviness of resentment in our hearts, our countenance, our speech, and our mood will be adversely affected.

Despite the fact that we may have been wronged by one or maybe a few individuals, everyone around us will begin to be affected. Resentment often causes us to be irritable, depressed, and generally very unpleasant. And to make matters worse, it is often the people we love and not the people that wronged us, who will end up suffering as a result of what took place.

The weight of resentment has also been known to affect our memory, productivity at work, ability to perform routine tasks, ability to focus, and even our sex drive. Being bitter, and refusing to forgive has also been linked to weakened immune systems, poor heart health, and even high blood pressure. As you can see, refusing to forgive will never prove beneficial.

But what exactly is forgiveness? Is it simply forgetting what took place? Does forgiveness means we simply pretend that nothing happened? Nope. It is not that simple. When we forgive, we must involve more than our words.

We must change how we think and feel about the individual. It is as if we are allowing them to start with a clean slate all over again. You refuse to allow the situation to cause you or the parties involved to hurt you any longer. This requires a high level of emotional intelligence, self-control, and love. Forgiveness is not just "letting them off the hook" for what they did, it is allowing those involved to stop dwelling in the past and move on to more important things.

"Forgiveness means that you fill yourself with love, and you radiate that love outward. You need to refuse to hang onto the venom or hatred that was engendered by the behaviors that caused the wounds." - Wayne Dyer

Becoming that enraged as a result of someone else's actions, and allowing yourself to remain upset over what took place for an extended period of time, is really giving the individual they keys to your happiness. It is as if you are allowing that individual to control you, and they will continue to control you until you muster up the courage needed to forgive them.

Forgiveness is also beneficial because it often results when we become aware of our own faults. It becomes easier for us to forgive when we remember that we too have had to ask for forgiveness many times. Contrary to what we may believe, we are not perfect. We sometimes hurt the people around us, even the ones we love, without even realizing it. When we refuse to harbor resentment and practice forgiveness, it will be easy for those around us to forgive us when we err.

Here are a few reasons why it is beneficial to practice being forgiving:

• You will be a lot happier and in a much better mood

• You will sleep better at night

• You will not jeopardize your job by not being productive

• You will not jeopardize your relationship with your significant other or your family

• You will learn greater self-control and self-awareness

• Your will enjoy greater peace

• You will gain the respect of those around you
• You will no longer feel the pain of the damage that was done

• You will experience less anxiety

• Your self-esteem will increase as you observe your own personal strength

What Forgiveness is Not!

Being forgiving does not mean you have to be a push over and allow yourself to be hurt over and over again. While you will let go of any grudge that you may have against the party or parties that wronged you, you certainly do not have to put yourself in a position for you to be hurt that way again. It is perfectly acceptable to be a little more cautious now that you have seen what these people are capable of. But, please be very careful. In the case of minor offenses, which are those that were not purposefully malicious, do not make the mistake of assuming that the act represents who the person is. Please remember that we all make mistakes, and we too have caused someone else pain.

Forgiveness is also not an opportunity for revenge. Declaring that you have forgiven someone is not a proclamation that you now have the "upper hand." The persons involved may have been guilty, but they certainly do not owe you anything. Even if they do not apologize, you have still gained quite a lot by extending this peace offering, and letting go of the bitterness that once
consumed you. Remember that by being forgiving, you are doing yourself a favor. While they might benefit as a result of your decision, forgiving them is actually a gift to yourself.

How to Forgive

Because we are both aware that forgiving someone who hurt you is not easy, I would never demand that you do so instantly or all at once. You have the option of forgiving in stages. Gradually letting go of your resentment towards the individuals who have wronged you, will ensure that you have enough time to root out any trace of the bitterness you have towards them, out of your mind and heart. If you get the opportunity to see this person often, you can start by simply saying hello.

This may come as a surprise to them because they were not expecting such a kind gesture, and that might open the way for the discussion you both need to get some closure. Sometimes, even though you were wronged, it is best to take the initiative to set matters straight. Always remember how this humble act will benefit you in the long run, whether they appreciate the gesture or not.

Another simple exercise that will help us to forgive is writing down the name of the person or persons that hurt you and listing all that they have ever done to upset you. Once you have completed that list, write a list of all the occasions on which you have hurt

someone, and had to ask for forgiveness. This is not something that we are inclined to think about. Seeing in black and white how often we have let our bad habits hurt those around us, especially those we love, may be just the push we need to let go of any grudges we may have. What is even more alarming to some individuals is when they see the names of the person they resent on the list of persons who they have had to ask for forgiveness.

Another useful exercise would be to make a list of all the good things this person has done for you. This exercise will help you to remember that despite their faults, this individual or these individuals, also have many beautiful qualities as well. In the case of those closest to us, these qualities are the very reason why we loved them and kept them close in the first place. Just think, extending the olive branch of peace may even help this person to see the flaw in their thinking and change for the better. You would have made the world a better place by helping just one individual to become a better person. Such kindness does not go unnoticed, or without reward.

It takes a very strong person to be forgiving. But think of how much better our lives would be if we did not walk around with the bitterness of resentment each day. Letting go of that heavy burden is one of the best ways to heal ourselves. This world was already a catastrophe, and it certainly does not need any more resentment to make it worse. The next chapter will explain how
being generous can also help us become far happier, and more successful people in this world, simply by being generous.

SIX

BE GENEROUS

"If you can't feed a hundred people, then just feed one."
—Mother Teresa

A generous person is not required to give all their possessions away. A generous person is also not required to allow others to push them around. Being generous involves firstly, the readiness to give or being willing to give more than is required.

Being generous takes kindness to the next level. You might be kind at heart, and often think about helping others, but unless you actually take them time to actually get the ball rolling in offering your time, energy or other resources for the benefit of another individual, you have not truly mastered the art of being generous. Generosity moves us to give of ourselves willingly, and expect nothing in return.

I know you should be wondering how giving away your assets can help you live a better life. The truth is that many often regard generosity of one of the keys to being truly happy in this miserable world. In fact, many medical practitioners will attest to the fact that being generous is also very good for your health. In fact, here are some of the proven benefits of giving generously:

- Reduced stress
- Lessening the likelihood of suffering from depression
- Increased sense of purpose
- Greater happiness
- Stronger families and marriages
- Less clutter
- Reduced risk of dementia
- Greater appreciation for all that you have
- More likely to benefit from the generosity of others

A generous person often seeks out opportunities to do good for others. Just think about volunteers who make their way to help out at Soup Kitchens every weekend. Those of us brave enough to sign up for the Peace Corps are also considered quite generous. But simply helping an elderly lady with her grocery bags, or stopping to allow a child to cross the road, can be considered generous. This kind of concern for others proves beneficial because it forces us to focus on the needs of others instead of on our own problems. Anything that minimizes the effect of our problems, whether in our relationships or even financially, will have a direct effect on our health. Being generous protects us from all the cynicism and narcissism that makes it so hard to navigate our way through this world.

I would, however, encourage you to be cautious as you endeavor to be more generous. Be very careful of the way in which you demonstrate your generosity. Please be especially careful when being generous to members of the opposite sex. If you are already taken, and you don't want to send the wrong impression, avoid gifts or favors that are personal in nature. A personal gift is anything related to one's body. Perfume, for example, would be considered a personal gift.

Please also bear in mind that your own safety may come into play when being generous. Many people have gotten robbed when asked by a seemingly homeless person to give some money. Reaching into your wallet or bag, and revealing where your cash is kept, and how much cash you have, is a bad idea, no matter how needy the person may appear to be. A safer option would be to let the person know that you will return with a gift.

I would strongly suggest that you go to a secure location, one that is away from prying eyes, and package everything that you would like to donate to this individual in advance. My final word of caution is that you need to feel out the person before being too generous. Some people like spontaneity and others prefer if you first ask them if they need your help. Even the best of intentions
can put you in awkward situations if they are not executed correctly.

We have discussed at length, how improving various aspects of your own personality can help you to heal yourself, and avoid a lot of the emotional baggage that comes along with the negativity in this world. The final of this book holds the most important key to healing all the scars caused by this nasty world. Please read on to learn more about what that is.

SEVEN
BE YOURSELF

"Be yourself; everyone else is already taken." — Oscar Wilde

"The greatest gift you ever give is your honest self." — Fred Rogers

We all need to learn to be ourselves again. This is one of the most crucial aspects of successfully navigating through this catastrophe we call life. This encouragement is in no way giving you the right to be a jerk. We have already discussed that healing ourselves from the pain caused by this world requires that we work hard to get rid of our negative traits.

Traits such as being arrogant, rude, dishonest and stingy have no place in your life. When we proudly walk around with these ugly habits, we are inviting all sorts of negativity into our lives. The result of that is only more pain and disappointment. That is why I encouraged you in the very first chapter to get to know yourself. This will better equip you to heal yourself, by learning more about your faults.

So what exactly does it mean to be yourself? It requires that you distance yourself from all the labels the world around us has imposed on us. These ugly labels come about because of the way
we look, the way we dress or even the community we grew up in. There is no reason for us to allow the world around us to squeeze us into a mold that doesn't really represent who we are. Just think about how liberating it would be to not have to pretend to be something you are not. This is all within reason of course. We would never want to take certain liberties that may have far- reaching effects on our personal life, and may even jeopardize our jobs. That means that you might want to hold off on anything drastic, like dying your hair purple and green, until you find an employer that is willing to accommodate such a choice.

Here are 5 important reasons why you need to start being true to yourself:

1. You will never be able to please everyone. If you constantly allow the people around you to determine who you are, you will constantly have to change what you stand for in order to try and make everyone happy. The only problem with this is that you will be dealing with so many conflicting demands that you will eventually end up disappointing someone. Additionally, putting yourself under this kind of pressure will leave you feeling dissatisfied in the end.

2. The society around us really doesn't know what it wants. The media portrays both the meek homemaker and the fierce go- getter, as the ideal woman. Society also demands that men be sensitive to the needs of the opposite sex and

the dangerous bad

boy as well. Which will you be if you are simply allowing those around you to determine who you are? Whatever you decide to be, just remember that it is quite exhausting to be putting on this kind of show every day.

3. You will end up making life-changing decisions based on the whims of the people around you, who will not suffer the consequences of these choices. If you decide to have a child, simply because your family thinks it's time, you will be the one to have to take care of that child! If you decide to pursue a career because your peers think you would do well in it, you will have to live with the burden of a career that you hate, forever.

4. The truth always comes out. Sooner or later, people will begin to realize that you are faking. Unfortunately, as we see in the case of many celebrities, the truth often comes out in a big scandal or breakdown.

5. When you are content with who you are, you will be truly happy. How can you love yourself, when you are constantly pretending to be something that you are not?

When all is said and done, you need to take control of your life if you want to see real improvements. You cannot expect different results if you are not bold enough to make drastic changes. And the time for those changes is now!

Conclusion

I hope you have benefitted from this book. By benefit, I mean that I hope you have decided to make some much need changes.

Progress may be slow at first, but you will never regret the decision to change yourself for the better. Every step, no matter how small, is a step forward, and can thus rightly be viewed as progress.

The universe has a way of rewarding the good in us and helping us to find the good in others.

By now, you should have realized that the secret to healing ourselves, and successfully navigating through the catastrophe of life, lies in our hands. Unless we acknowledge our own faults, and actively work to try and improve on them, our lives will never get any better.

"As human beings, our greatness lies not so much in being able to remake the world - that is the myth of the atomic age - as in being able to remake ourselves." — Mahatma Gandhi